Dedication

To Richard, life mentor, who has helped open up life's
possibilities for me.

Contents

Introduction

This book attempts to reveal some of the structural complexities involved in implementing authentic cooperative learning in the classroom. The book reveals that cooperative learning is far more than putting students into groups and letting them work on their own. It also suggests that when full cooperative learning structures are implemented, the benefits in student achievement often can be astounding.

This book has four main sections. Section one, titled *Description*, offers definitions and research background about cooperative learning. For those with little experience in cooperative learning, this section gives a helpful overview.

Section two, titled *Decisions*, reviews the many areas to consider as one contemplates initiating cooperative learning in the classroom. This section provides a helpful checklist even for those who have already embarked on using cooperative learning.

Section three, titled *Designs*, offers many cooperative learning structures for use in any classroom, in any grade level, in any content area. By dividing those structures into whole class, pair, and triad/quad units, the teacher can see the many choices and possibilities for using cooperative learning.

Finally, section four, titled *Developments*, suggests the social skill benefits that can result when cooperative learning is carried out well in the classroom. The areas of communication, team building, consensus generation, and leadership can all be greatly enhanced by appropriate uses of cooperative learning. The underlying implication of this section is to show that social skills are crucial if cooperative learning is to succeed. Often, the consequences of this is that social skills need to be taught directly at first to make sure students are clear about what is involved in specific social skills.

My hope is that all four of these sections together provide enough interest and practical tools to enable anyone to risk initiating cooperative learning. My hope is that when cooperative learning is well implemented, student learning achievement will soar.

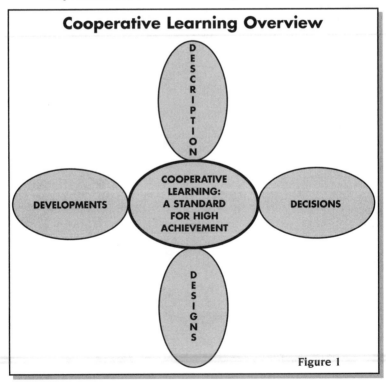

Figure 1

Description

Mr. Dowling stood up, for it was his turn to share what he had been doing with cooperative learning since the training four weeks ago. All eyes were on him, because everyone knew that he was an experienced high school teacher who wanted nothing of this "Cooperative Learning." Everyone's mouth dropped as he proudly displayed several graphic organizers his cooperative learning groups had created during a lesson. Almost as intriguing and impressive as the student work was his own excitement as he described the eagerness of his students to work in groups and his pleasure at how much they had learned.

Definition

"*Cooperative learning* is the instructional use of small groups so that students work together to maximize their own and others' learning" (Johnson, Johnson, & Holubec, 1998, p. 1.5). When it is done well, cooperative learning is a highly structured teaching strategy that capitalizes on the fact that many children learn better in the midst of interaction with their peers. Robert Slavin (1987) suggested that cooperative learning occurs when instructional methods enable students to work and learn in small, heterogeneous-ability groups. When this happens, cooperative learning is able to lead students into the "social power of learning" (Zemelman, Daniels, & Hyde, 1993).

Furthermore, cooperative learning enables skills in working as teams, skills that are in dire demand in the workplace. The SCANS report of April, 1992 (U. S. Department of Labor, pp. 81–2), lists five crucial workplace competencies: resources, interpersonal, information, systems, and technology. The report suggests the following interpersonal skills are needed for today's workplace: Participates as a member of a team, teaches others, serves clients/customers, exercises leadership, negotiates to arrive at a decision, and works with cultural diversity. All of these are enhanced through cooperative learning.

Does it work? Johnson, Johnson, and Holubec (1998) cite more than 550 experimental and 100 correlational studies that conclude that there is an increase in academic achievement, more positive and collaborative interpersonal relationships, and greater self-esteem.

Small group work compared to cooperative learning group work is often highly unstructured. With the absence of a clearly defined task and a designated group task, small group work may flounder. Sometimes, only one student in the group does the work, and it may be difficult to discern which student did which part of the work. Quality varies dramatically without clear images of what is to be accomplished. This kind of small group work leaves students, teachers, and parents highly frustrated.

In cooperative learning groups, the task is clearly and definitively structured. The goals of the task are thoroughly explained. If the project is major, the pieces of the project are parceled out to specific individuals so that it is clear who does what in the final product. Because the group is heterogeneous, the complex task calls on the strengths and abilities of everyone in the group to complete. In this way, the learning experience becomes interactive and exciting.

What Does Cooperative Learning Look Like?

What can it look like? Math teachers assign different math problems to different groups. After a problem is solved, a group can teach it to other groups. Social studies teachers divide the country into regions, asking each group to prepare a structured group presentation on the region for everyone. Language arts teachers assign different acts of a play to groups to perform for the entire class. Science teachers ask groups to create solutions to environmental issues and present them to the class. Elementary teachers ask different groups in a class to study and present material on different Indian tribes in the country.

All of this is in lieu of students merely reading the material, listening to a lecture by the teacher, and, finally, regurgitating the information back to the teacher on a paper-pencil test. A well-functioning classroom mixes individual and cooperative teaching strategies so that the more solitary person becomes comfortable with team situations and the more gregarious person becomes comfortable with individual learning tasks.

Elements: R.I.C.H.E.S.

R.I.C.H.E.S. is a useful acronym to serve as a guideline for the requisite elements of effective cooperative learning. It reflects the research and the large amount of practical material developed through the years in the area of cooperative learning. Starting with Johnson, Johnson, and Holubec's five elements—positive interdependence, individual and group accountability, face-to-face interaction, interpersonal and small group skills, and group processing—R.I.C.H.E.S. blends two other elements—higher order thinking and the emotional realm—to present six cooperative learning elements:

Reflection
Individual Achievement
Collaboration
Higher Order Thinking
Emotional Realm
Social Skills.

Figure 2 illustrates these elements. When all six of these elements are integrated into a lesson flow, students have a vehicle for motivated and interactive learning. All six of these elements are absolutely necessary for true cooperative learning to occur. Let's look at each individually.

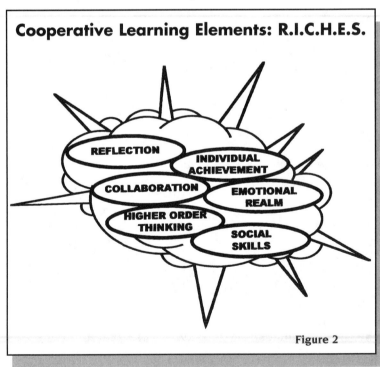

Cooperative Learning Elements: R.I.C.H.E.S.

REFLECTION
INDIVIDUAL ACHIEVEMENT
COLLABORATION
EMOTIONAL REALM
HIGHER ORDER THINKING
SOCIAL SKILLS

Figure 2

Reflection

> ...teachers may expend a great deal of effort in orchestrating an experience, only to discover that students have absorbed very little. Educators, therefore, need to deliberately work with students to help them more fully benefit from their experiences.

> We call this aspect of brain-based learning active processing. *It is the consolidation and internalization of information, by the learner, in a way that is both personally meaningful and conceptually coherent.* It is the path to understanding, rather than simply to memory. (Caine & Caine, 1991, p. 147, italics in original).

Through their research on learning and the brain, the Caines reveal the significant role of reflection or processing in helping information become meaningful to the student. Reflection provides a chance for the brain to create meaning out of what has just been encountered. It is often in these moments of reflection and processing that information is connected, for the first time, to previously learned material or previously created conceptual frameworks.

Perhaps asking a closing question engenders the connection—for example, "How does what we have looked at today connect with the work we did last week on _____?" Class responses to this question can help students make additional sense out of the lesson just finished. Or, perhaps the connection is fostered by a four-minute opportunity to write in a journal—for example, "Summarize in your journal three key insights you have about our lesson today." Whatever it is, it does not need to take a lot of time.

Individual Achievement

> To be a cooperative group, each member must be held accountable to learn the assigned material and help other group members learn. Individual accountability results in group members knowing they cannot 'hitch-hike' on the work of others, loaf, or get a free ride. (Johnson, Johnson, & Holubec, 1998, p. 4.17)

The classic proponents of cooperative learning, including Johnson, Johnson, and Holubec, all agree that individual achievement is the bottom line of well-structured cooperative learning. Cooperative learning calls on the teacher to construct the tasks in such a way that individual accountability is possible and practical, even within a group project, performance, or presentation.

This may mean, at one time, allowing learning to happen cooperatively, followed by an individual assignment in which each person demonstrates his or her learning; or, at other times, breaking down a project into sections for which individuals are primarily responsible. However accountability is done, it is imperative to gather evidence of what each individual student has learned. One of the common criticisms of cooperative learning by both students and parents is that often a teacher gives a group grade that does not reflect the differing skills and knowledge levels of the students in the cooperative learning group. Group grades are not recommended because they create unnecessary barriers to implementing cooperative learning successfully.

Collaboration

Unite the class so students form bonds of trust, which enable teamwork. (Bellanca & Fogarty, 1991, p. 3)

It is indispensable to the success of cooperative learning for team members to bond and connect. It may be a common task that brings individuals together as a team, or it may be creating a team name, flag, or motto that elicits that sense of team. Sometimes, real unity emerges because the task is so challenging that it demands every team member's thinking and working to succeed. Many teachers assign roles to each student in a group to enable the team to grow as a cohesive unit. Over time and with practice, collaboration becomes second nature to students.

Yet, successful teams do not just happen. Much depends on how the teacher has helped teamwork to grow, step by step, in the class. Growing strong teams is as complex a process as teaching a confusing and difficult scientific concept. It takes time. Teachers can't expect students to understand in September what they will gradually grasp about cooperative learning and teamwork by April.

Higher Order Thinking

The vision of education as the development of critical thinking abilities is evident as students deliberate and persevere in their problem solving, as they work to make their oral and written work more precise and accurate, as they consider others' points of view, as they generate questions, and as they explore the alternatives and consequences of their actions. (Costa, 1991, p. 13)

Although data and information are still a critical part of what needs to be learned in one's journey through school, learning how to think and becoming aware of how one thinks are also integral parts of what a student needs to learn. Using critical thinking to resolve issues and solve problems is becoming another attribute that employers look for in new employees (U. S. Department of Labor, 1992, pp. 83–4). Furthermore, as data and information exponentially increase, as older data and information constantly and rapidly become obsolete and are replaced, the skills of making judgments and discerning the essential and critical information are becoming more crucial for the well-prepared student.

In the classroom, encouraging higher order thinking looks like a teacher inquiring how a student reached a conclusion rather than stopping the interaction after the student gives a response to a problem. In math, it means asking students how they arrived at particular solutions. In language arts, it means asking what values a student used in picking a character in the novel as the main character. In science, it means posing a problem for student inquiry. In this way, the classroom becomes as much process oriented as content and product oriented (Fogarty, 1991, p. 7).

Emotional Realm

What factors are at play, for example, when people of high IQ flounder and those of modest IQ do surprisingly well? I would argue that the difference quite often lies in the abilities called here *emotional intelligence*, which include self-control, zeal and persistence, and the ability to motivate oneself.

In recent years, research has shown that emotions play a crucial role in the classroom. Because some students come from emotion-starved existences, it is vital to allow classrooms to be places of rich emotions. Consequently, emotional education cannot happen by chance (Goleman, 1995, p. xiii).

Some of this emotional education occurs as emotional bonds are created among the students themselves; some as emotional bonds are nurtured between teacher and students. Emotional education also occurs as feelings are acknowledged relative to emotion-laden topics discussed in class. Sometimes, just posing questions that allow emotions to be felt and expressed is all that is necessary to bring the emotional realm into the classroom. When teachers do this, they acknowledge that emotions are the source of motivation for learning. In other words, driving out emotion from a classroom essentially drives out motivation. Allowing emotion into the classroom in structured and healthy ways allows the possibility of learning motivation to deepen.

In addition to this, as schools raise concerns about character education, research is suggesting that the emotional capacities are at the heart of developing mature ethical approaches in life (Goleman, 1995, p. xii). Deepening one's awareness of one's own and others' emotions awakens the capacity of ethical concerns and responses. This suggests that limiting emotional awareness also curtails ethical awareness.

Social Skills

Cooperative learning is inherently more complex than competitive or individualistic learning because students have to engage simultaneously in taskwork and teamwork. Group members must know how to provide effective leadership, decision-making, trust-building, communication, and conflict-management, and be motivated to use the prerequisite skills. You have to teach teamwork skills just as purposefully and precisely as you do academic skills. (Johnson, Johnson, & Holubec, 1998, p. 1.14)

If students are to work together in task groups rather than working individually sitting at desks arranged in rows, then the need for social skills is apparent immediately. In an age of television and computers, educators cannot assume that every student understands even basic social skills such as listening when others talk, taking turns, encouraging others, using appropriate voice levels, and so on. It would be nice if students came to class already practicing these social skills. However, given the realities of the actual level of social skills present in most students, teachers need to offer instruction in social skills and then reinforce that instruction by allowing the skills to be practiced and used over and over again in the classroom.

Bringing R.I.C.H.E.S. to the classroom means bringing reflection, individual achievement, collaboration, higher order thinking, emotional realm, and social skills into the teaching process as fundamental elements for cooperative learning. When integrated well into classroom lessons, these six elements provide the needed structures for cooperative learning to flourish. In addition, although these elements encourage the individual student to even higher levels of academic achievement, they also foster the skills for life-long learning.

Research

A review of research focuses on two approaches: theory and practice. Figure 3 recaps the research sources discussed in this section.

Research Overview

Theory   **Practice**

Bellanca & Fogarty, 1991   Slavin, 1991

Johnson, Johnson, &   Schneidewind &
Holubec, 1986, 1998   Davidson, 2000

Slavin, 1987, 1989, 1991

Kagan, 1989

Sharan & Sharan (cited in
Bellanca & Fogarty, 1991)

Figure 3

Theory

Johnson, Johnson, and Holubec (1986) laid the foundations of cooperative learning theory. They emphasized five essential elements to cooperative learning groups: positive interdependence, individual and group accountability, face-to-face interaction, interpersonal and small group skills, and group processing.

In turn, Robert Slavin (1987, 1989, 1991) took the principles of cooperative learning and packaged them with curriculum to use in a cooperative approach. Team Accelerated Instruction is a mathematics program. Cooperative Integrated Reading and

Composition is a language arts curriculum particularly for early grades. By creating these curriculum packages, Slavin removes many obstacles for teachers who don't immediately see how to integrate cooperative learning with curricula.

Spencer Kagan (1989) is noted for creating a number of structures, such as the jigsaw and the round robin, that can be applied to any curricula.

Finally, Bellanca and Fogarty (1991) call attention to Shlomo Sharan and Yael Sharan's contribution of the Group Investigative Model. The model uses five stages: (1) posing the big question and forming groups by interest, (2) identifying the inquiry problem and defining the research process, (3) dividing up the work in order to gather the needed data and information, (4) drawing up the report, and finally, (5) presenting and assessing the report. In closing, Bellanca and Fogarty lay out their own approach to cooperative learning, which emphasizes higher order thinking tasks. In their approach, the cooperative learning group is a productive milieu in which to intensify the cognitive.

For one of the best reviews of educational research done on cooperative learning theory, see Bellanca and Fogarty, *Blueprints for Thinking in the Cooperative Classroom* (1991).

Practice

A great deal of research has analyzed the effectiveness of cooperative learning in the classroom. When cooperative learning is carried out well, research overwhelmingly suggests that cooperative learning improves student academic achievement. A more comprehensive discussion of benefits follows this section.

Slavin notes two elements—group goals and individual accountability—that must occur for effective cooperative learning (1991, p. 105). In other words, when the sense of team is heightened (Collaboration) and appropriate means of checking individual learning are included, individual achievement soars.

This is not all that the research suggests. Positive impacts show up in areas of self-esteem, in relating to others, and in attitudes toward the school itself (Slavin, 1991, p. 100). Today, cooperative learning is seen as a most effective tool for differentiated learning. "But when teachers implement cooperative learning thoughtfully and differentiate tasks within it, they can personalize student learning, help students collaborate while challenging each individual in the context of a group effort, and encourage students to appreciate their peers' diverse competencies and experiences" (Schniedewind & Davidson, 2000, p. 24).

In other words, when carried out well, cooperative learning can help students academically, socially, and emotionally. Research backs up improvement in academic achievement, even in paper-pencil tests and standardized tests. Students learn new social skills in relating to each other in supportive ways. On the emotional level, student self-esteem rises. The key is the caveat that these improvements occur when cooperative learning is done well.

Benefits

Individual

Already, it is clear that when cooperative learning is implemented well, individual students see huge benefits. For many students, academic achievement is distinctly enhanced. Slavin summarized 67 studies about student achievement and cooperative learning (1991, p. 76). Of these studies, 61% showed significant academic achievement in using cooperative learning. Also, there appeared to be significant improvements in a student's sense of self-worth. Teachers say that many lost and confused students find their way and improve their sense of self as they become significantly engaged in a cooperative learning group in the classroom. Finally, there are real changes in the way students treat each other the more they are exposed to cooperative learning. When cooperative learning is done well, teachers report that the need for discipline referrals dramatically declines. At the same time, students have learned positive ways to communicate with other students.

Classroom

When the class has been well trained in cooperative learning structures, the teacher is able to move around the class and target individuals or groups needing extra attention. The classroom turns into an action research laboratory where the buzz of exploration and excitement can be felt. Some classrooms become rainforest jungles as student groups create different aspects of the jungle, and others become oceans when oceanography is studied. Still others are transformed into 16th century English cottages or castles as Shakespearean plays are studied. Now, the teacher manages several teams engaged in various aspects of the task, rather than monitoring 30 individuals.

School

It is most helpful to individual teachers when cooperative learning is used throughout the school. In these schools, students show up for classes at the beginning of the year already familiar with many cooperative learning approaches. This means that when teachers assign roles for cooperative groups, students already know what the roles are. When teachers refer to certain social skills, students are familiar with them. As students become more and more familiar with working in cooperative groups, they become more willing to accept responsibility for their own learning.

The challenge of all teachers in schools where the students are familiar with cooperative learning is to keep altering the tasks, the structures, and the methods used so that students don't become bored with cooperative learning.

Again, cooperative learning calls for a high degree of communication and planning among the teachers to make sure that each unit comes across in a fresh and challenging way.

Community

A classroom in which cooperative learning is practiced successfully can become a laboratory for cooperation rather than a place that fosters individual hostilities and competitive mindsets. Consequently, the cooperative classroom lives and breathes a sense of community. In this way, students are encouraged to become aware of people's strengths and gifts. In this way, diversity is strengthened.

Some teachers have used cooperative learning groups for service learning projects. Cleaning up a river bed, transforming an unused lot into a place of beauty, or interviewing the elderly in nursing homes can have a huge impact on the community. This opens new ways for the community and the schools to communicate with one another. Needless to say, as this spirit is strengthened, the local community feels the difference when schools become places that model how to work together.

Workplace

Businesses seek employees who know how to get along with others and how to work together in teams. Businesses have found that complex tasks require the concerted effort of teams. Whether at a university, on a factory floor, in a hospital, or within a large corporation, many tasks are carried out by teams. Well-implemented cooperative learning lays the groundwork for developing employees who are comfortable working in teams, sharing the workload, or supporting each other as team members. When students and parents ask why students have to work in cooperative learning groups, there is sound reason to encourage the reluctant cooperative learning participant to join in.

Decisions

A pre-K to 12th grade Academy decided to change how it would structure the school and teach in the classroom. The administration and faculty began with a two-day strategic planning workshop to pull together their vision and their plan for carrying out their vision. Soon after, they engaged in a rigorous professional development program to train the teachers in cooperative learning and other strategies. The consultant came back repeatedly to add more training and to evaluate what was actually going on in the classrooms. Many thoughtful decisions came into play (planning, training, monitoring, supporting) as they carried out their plans to change the structure and teaching of their Academy.

Teachers need to consider six main areas when approaching cooperative learning for their classrooms: communication, physical tools, group formation, lesson supports, management tactics, and success monitoring (Figure 4).

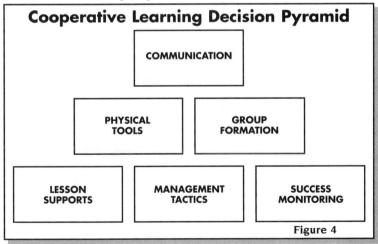

Cooperative Learning Decision Pyramid

COMMUNICATION

PHYSICAL TOOLS

GROUP FORMATION

LESSON SUPPORTS

MANAGEMENT TACTICS

SUCCESS MONITORING

Figure 4

Each area has a specific focus. *Communication* reminds one that it may be wise to check with some crucial people before initiating plans for cooperative learning. *Physical tools* reviews some of the important "props" to gather before starting cooperative learning projects. *Group formation* gives hints and suggestions as to how to form cooperative learning groups. *Lesson supports* offers some points for planning cooperative learning lessons. *Management tactics* considers necessary support for initiating cooperative learning. Finally, *success monitoring* raises the question of assessment and accountability in the cooperative learning milieu.

Communication

Keeping key people aware of what teachers are doing in their cooperative learning classrooms is crucial. Cooperative administrators are vital to supporting this communication effort. Helping parents understand the rationale behind cooperative learning before beginning removes negative issues that could come up later. Finally, raising students' interest and expectations for cooperative learning helps the entire transition.

Administration

It is crucial to give early information to people in the school community about plans to initiate cooperative learning. First and foremost, teachers need to let their administrator in on their plans; this is strategic commonsense. There are three possible reactions from an administrator. The first and most likely is that an administrator will be supportive, which is very helpful. The second is that an administrator may be questioning or unsure; then it is doubly important to proceed in a way that brings the administrator on board, eventually gaining his or her support. The third and least desirable response is that an administrator is passive about the idea, and, although not supportive, does not put obstacles in the way.

Most Frequently Asked Questions About Cooperative Learning

1. What's wrong with the traditional way of teaching?

   Nothing is wrong with it. However, many students are not learning in the traditional way. I am suggesting an approach that uses a number of different ways of teaching to meet the needs of students that learn in different ways.

2. What is the ideal group size?

   The ideal group size is three or four. Size might depend, however, on where the class is in their familiarity with cooperative learning.

3. What do you do when a student won't participate?

   First of all, I want to explore the real reasons why the student won't participate. It may that the student is being ridiculed by classmates or there may be some home issues. At first, I might just make sure the student is responsible on his or her own for getting all the work done. Gradually, I would see if the student would work with me, the teacher. Then, I might see if the student would work with one other student, and so on.

4. Isn't the teacher the expert who should be doing the teaching?

   The teacher is still doing the teaching because the teacher is closely monitoring everything that is going on. The teacher is doing the teaching through the use of the entire class to provide explicit input needed for the cooperative group work.

5. How do kids teach each other?

Kids teach each other in practically the same way that adults teach kids. They talk, show, demonstrate, and explain. In fact, teachers will tell you that sometimes a student says exactly what the teacher has been saying over and over again, but because it is a fellow student the other student hears it correctly for the first time.

6. Suppose kids are teaching the wrong information to others? Again, this calls for close monitoring by the teacher. During cooperative learning tasks, the teacher is not sitting at the teacher's desk doing other work. The teacher is moving around listening to all the conversations and making sure that correct information is being shared.

7. How do you prevent one student from doing all the work?

By carefully structured assignments, by well-chosen roles in the group, the teacher can make sure that all students are engaged in the assignment. Often, by breaking down the assignment and giving a piece to each person in the group, it is possible to determine who has done what.

8. How do you grade? (Do you give group grades?)

Although many teachers have found a way to make group grades work, I strongly recommend that only individual grades be given—especially at the early stages of cooperative learning. Group grades are often one of the most contentious practices in cooperative learning. The learning can be cooperative; the assessment can be individual.

Figure 5

Parents

Parents definitely need some explanation of new cooperative learning plans. Many parents have heard of cooperative learning, and some may have developed negative opinions about it (Figure 5). One big concern is the whole area of group grades. It disturbs both parents and students that the child's grades might be lowered by the performance of others on the child's team. This is one reason not to give group grades. Simply grade individual efforts and results. Assuring the parents of this policy relieves a lot of anxiety.

Another concern is that one student in the group will end up doing all the work on any given project. To prevent this, teachers structure the task in such a way that they know exactly who is doing what. Again, the principle of "individual achievement" is important here, and parental reassurance of this is vital. Consider demonstrating a cooperative learning lesson during an Open House to give parents a first-hand feel for structured group learning.

Another method for reassuring parents is to send a simple letter that introduces plans to move to cooperative learning. Giving parents information about cooperative learning reduces their fears and anxieties about it. Figure 6 shows a letter sent by one teacher.

Letter To Parents Introducing Cooperative Learning

Dear Parent,

I would like to share with you one of the "best practices" I will be using in your child's classroom. You and I are both concerned that students achieve at their maximum abilities. That is why a portion of classroom time will feature students learning and working together in small, highly structured groups.

In other words, in addition to time spent in the classroom in very traditional settings, there will also be time spent in these cooperative learning groups. Some children learn better in more traditional, individualized settings, but other children learn better in more interactive, collaborative settings. But, in life, both kinds of interactions are needed, thus both sets of skills need to be practiced.

Perhaps you have some questions. Please call me; my number is (telephone number). In addition, I am demonstrating a cooperative learning lesson after school on October 5th from 4 to 5 p.m. and will offer the same demonstration lesson at our school's Open House on the evening of October 7 from 7 to 8 p.m. I will be available for your questions after each of these demonstrations.

Thank you for your interest and support.

Name

Figure 6

Students

Finally, it goes without saying that teachers need to prepare their students for this shift in how some of the learning will happen in the classroom. Talking to students about how group work will proceed helps them to anticipate cooperative learning. A bulletin board might help to focus the conversation about cooperative learning. Doing some simple brief work in pairs is another way to prepare students. Getting their input on what some of the class ground rules might be is another way to attract their support. When cooperative learning is done well, students are a teacher's best allies.

Physical Tools

Good cooperative learning does not just happen. Any lesson, whether cooperative or not, requires preparation. Some lessons require materials or "props." Let's look at three of these physical props: room arrangement, the teacher's materials, and the students' materials.

Room Arrangement

The arrangement of the classroom can be conducive to carrying out cooperative learning. If using teams of three or four students, then design the classroom with tables or desks arranged in threes or fours. Although some teachers may think they do not have enough space to rearrange the desks, it is a fact that desks arranged in rows is the least economical way to use space. Be sure to allow room for the teacher to walk around the classroom.

Find a place to store materials and keep in mind the need for one or more learning centers in the room as the classroom is set up.   Again, this is another opportunity to involve students: get them to help lay out the classroom.

A short anecdote points up the impact of room arrangement. When I visited a parochial school classroom taught by a 72-year-old sister, I immediately noticed that the chairs and desks were arranged in groups of four.   Although I have no evidence that she was using all of the structures of cooperative learning, I could immediately see that she was inviting students to talk to each other.

Teacher Materials

Think through ahead of time precisely what materials are needed to carry out a lesson. The entire drama of a lesson can be sacrificed if the lesson is interrupted while the teacher looks for materials. Likewise, plan on using materials known to be available.   Being realistic saves wasted energy and needless anxiety. Concentrate on what's on hand and not on what might have been nice to include.

Materials teachers find helpful to have on hand for cooperative learning tasks are shown in Figure 7.

Materials for Cooperative Learning Tasks

Butcher paper or chart paper

Markers

Masking tape

3 X 5 cards

5 X 8 cards

Sticky notes

Colored paper

Scissors

Rulers

Figure 7

Student Materials

Everything said for teacher materials also applies to student materials. Some teachers collect students' materials in plastic bags or plastic boxes ahead of time, and also use these to store the materials between sessions. Having prepared the materials ahead of time allows the lesson to flow smoothly and also lets the teacher focus on how well the groups are functioning.

Group Formation

In cooperative learning, creating student groups is a critical decision. There are times when a group of two is needed. At other times, a group of three or four is more effective. Sometimes, groups can be formed quite randomly and spontaneously. At other times, especially for tasks or projects that will take a long time, careful thought needs to be used when forming groups.

Group Size

Many teachers wonder how to determine an effective group size. One factor in this process is to consider how comfortable class members are with cooperative learning. If at the beginning of the comfort scale, teachers may want to have a group no larger than two. As the students' comfort level increases, then increase the size of the group. In other words, it may be helpful to start with just pairs, graduate to groups of three, and then go on to groups of four or perhaps even five. The Johnsons prefer three as the optimal group size, whereas Kagan prefers four. Kagan's use of four allows the teacher to split the four into two pairs at certain points in the lesson.

Another factor in effective group size is the nature of the assignment. If students are to meet in a group for 20 or 30 minutes, three might be a good number. If students are dealing with a more extensive project with a great deal of complexity, a team of four or five might be justified. This factor calls for careful analysis of the task. Teachers want a match of task and group size that keeps everyone thoroughly engaged. It is important to keep in mind that when groups are too big, it's easier for some students to "drop out." At this point, discipline may become a problem.

Still another factor in this process may be the size of the room and the total number of students present. A classroom with 30 students may not allow physically for ten groups with comfort but might accommodate seven or eight groups.

Heterogeneous Grouping

Another question that is often asked is how to go about creating effective groupings of students. The key to this seems to be heterogeneity.

"As a rule, cooperative groups should contain low-, medium-, and high-ability students to help promote discussion, peer teaching, and justification of answers" (Johnson, Johnson, & Holubec, 1986, p. 29). Although this team refers to low, medium, and high abilities, heterogeneity also can be discussed in terms of differing multiple intelligences (visual/spatial, logical/mathematical, verbal/linguistic, musical/rhythmic, bodily/kinesthetic, interpersonal/social, intrapersonal/introspective, and naturalist). In other words, mixing intelligence strengths and gifts allows the group to experience the value of diversity.

This diversity calls for a wise creation of the task given to the groups—it creates a need for tasks that demand a variety of strengths in order to be completed successfully. In other words, giving a reading assignment to a group calls on only those in the group skilled at reading. However, assigning a reading followed by creating a graphic organizer, a pictorial representation, or a dramatic presentation also calls on those with other gifts and strengths in order to complete the task successfully.

Group Processing Methods

One key to successful group formation and group maturity is the opportunity to reflect on how the group is working together. Therefore, questions about group processing are a vital part of the life of group work. These can be simple questions (see Figure 8) that give group members some reflection time, an opportunity to applaud themselves, and the chance to analyze how they can work more helpfully in the future.

A Few Suggestions To Help Groups Reflect on Their Work Together

Rate yourself from one to ten relative to how well you worked as a team.

Talk about what things you did to support everyone's learning the assignment today.

How might you improve your performance as a group in the future?

Figure 8

Lesson Supports

Several things need to be considered as the teacher creates a cooperative learning lesson. Different lessons need to embody different strategies because students will tire of cooperative learning if every lesson looks the same. Furthermore, tasks need to be well defined and clearly structured. Last, assigning every person in the group a role within the structured task helps to engage every student in the lesson.

Variety of Strategies

To begin with, teachers find it helpful to have a variety of teaching strategies at their fingertips. Using the same strategy, cooperative learning lesson after cooperative learning lesson, will wear rather quickly on both teacher and students. The skilled cooperative learning teacher varies how groups are formed, which graphic organizers are used, which higher order thinking skills are emphasized, which social skills are highlighted, and what kind of products are to be created. The Bibliography includes a number of resources to expand a teacher's strategy repertoire.

Structured Tasks

Giving clearly defined tasks to the groups is extremely important. Hazy, confusing tasks bring a rapid rise in the noise level of the group as students continually poll each other trying to figure out what the real assigned task is.

For example, a teacher might say: "Please read this chapter and prepare a report to give the rest of the students." This is vague and unclear. But, if a teacher says, more helpfully: "After each of you read this chapter, please prepare a report as a group. The report needs to include five team insights from this chapter and three implications of these insights for society. Let's all be prepared to give the reports in 35 minutes." Note how specific the assignment and time allotment are in the second example.

Knowing exactly what level of task complexity to give groups is another important issue. Tasks that are too easy do not demand the thinking of everyone in the group and may lead to boredom or discipline issues. Tasks that are too complex overwhelm the group and may cause the group to give up immediately. Giving the group a simple worksheet to fill out usually is not a sufficient cooperative learning task. On the other hand, asking the group to fill out a graphic organizer on 10 articles within a class period probably asks too much.

Team Roles

Assigning group roles ahead of time is a tactic many teachers of cooperative learning find to be an effective start for teamwork. The roles actually used depend on the grade level or the subject being taught, of course. Some common roles are shown in Figure 9. Language arts teachers often add the Editor as another role. Mathematics teachers find the Calculator and Checker roles helpful. Assigning everyone a role keeps everyone engaged. Rotating roles among team members has several advantages: one person does not dominate the group as the constant leader, leadership skills are enhanced through responsibility, different multiple intelligences are engaged, and students' have opportunities to strengthen less-developed skills.

Management Tactics

Some Useful Group Roles

Organizer

Encourager

Recorder

Materials Handler

Reporter

Time Keeper

Checker

Figure 9

The area of management tactics includes clues to managing the classroom as a whole. These are suggestions to smooth out bumps in the implementation of cooperative learning.

Managing Tools

Managing a class that has seven or eight groups working at once is a very different classroom dynamic from managing 30 students sitting in rows while the teacher lectures. Particularly noticeable is the difference in the noise level in the room. When seven or eight groups are working in the same room, the noise level is higher. Exactly how high that level ends up really depends on the teacher.

In order to manage this factor, some teachers use signals. For example, some teachers use a raised hand followed by all the students raising their hands as a signal to return to a whole classroom focus with silence. Others ring a bell to signal that it is time to focus as a whole group and quiet down. Other teachers have created a hand signal that means "Keep working but tone down the noise." Some flip the light off and on to signal time to pay attention as a whole class.

In time and with consistent use, following these signals becomes second nature. Consider letting the students suggest if and what signals are needed for classroom cooperation, get them to design the signals, and add them to class guidelines, discussed next, as well.

Class Guidelines

As this difference in dynamic becomes clear, that is, that a cooperative learning classroom is often busier and more fragmented than the traditional classroom, teachers need to work with the class to create guidelines that help the class manage itself. Figure 10 shows some possible guidelines. Posting these guidelines in the room is a simple and direct way to make them available to everyone. In fact, posting allows the student groups themselves to refer to them if a member is getting out of hand.

Classroom Guidelines

One person speaks at a time.

Put-ups are expected; put-downs are not helpful.

Disagree with ideas, not with personalities.

Use small voices in groups, large voices for the class.

Everyone needs a chance to participate.

Figure 10

Targeted Social Skills

In this time of television, computers, high mobility, and demanding parental work schedules, many students show up at school needing help with social skills. Even saying please and thank-you may be a stretch for some. It is certain that taking turns and eliminating put-downs, to say nothing of conflict-resolving skills, are not natural to many students. In fact, it may seem that there are 20 or 30 social skills that teachers wish their students embodied. Although social skill development is discussed in more detail in the final chapter, it is important to consider desirable skills during the decision phase of implementing cooperative learning.

If a teacher considers the area of social skills as subject matter content, it is immediately obvious that all social skills can't be taught at once. A workable plan is to phase instruction or practice of these skills. Decide which four or five of the many desirable skills need to be emphasized and practiced first (Figure 11). Again, posting these skills somewhere in the room allows immediate access and reference when needed. As the class becomes proficient in the first set of skills, move on to the next-most desirable set on the list.

Desirable Social Skills for Cooperative Learning		
Taking turns	Listening attentively	Using small voices
Encouraging	Sharing	Including all
Helping each other	Respecting opinions	Clarifying opinions
Paraphrasing ideas	Creating options	Offering own ideas
Building on ideas	Honoring feelings	Integrating ideas

Figure 11

Success Monitoring

Monitoring success covers the area of assessing and evaluating individual and group progress. Learning achievement and growth is documented and celebrated. How to assess needs must be thought through ahead of time.

Individual Accountability

As has been mentioned already, individual accountability mechanisms are crucial for the success of cooperative learning. As the name cooperative learning implies, learning can be done in cooperative settings when appropriate. However, in general, accountability needs to be done individually, at least most of the time.

For example, a group creates a graphic organizer as a team. Individuals then write on that organizer individually. (Some teachers provide different color markers for each of the students in the group so that the teacher can discern which student wrote which contributions in the organizer.) The project has sections written by individuals to show each individual's accomplishment. Tests and quizzes are given following the group learning. Finally, individual grades are recorded, just as in traditional class work.

Group Accountability

Although the emphasis has been on individual accountability, there are ways that the teacher can keep tabs on how groups are functioning and working together. Sometimes, observation checklists give the teacher documentation on how well groups are doing. At other times, teachers ask group members to rate themselves on how well they are working together. Group presentations also reveal how a group has been working together. All of these give the teacher evidence and documentation as to the group's operating cohesion and effectiveness. This evidence can be the basis of group conferences.

Rewards, Incentives, Celebrations

One decision a teacher makes according to his or her own philosophy of teaching is whether to reward individuals or teams for participation in their groups. Simple things like stickers or stars sometimes go a long way. For example, when changing how teaching is done, such as when introducing cooperative learning, rewards and incentives might be appropriate to acknowledge the good work going on.

If rewards and incentives do not fit a teacher's philosophy (and there is some good thinking that says rewards and incentives do not help in the classroom), perhaps occasional celebrations might communicate how well a class is implementing cooperative learning. Rewards and incentives could include seeing a movie, extending recess time, having a few minutes for game time, reading a story, serving food, or whatever else says to students, Good job!

Figure 12 recaps the decisions needed to get started with cooperative learning.

Decisions for Getting Started with Cooperative Learning					
Communi-cation	Physical Tools	Group Formation	Lesson Supports	Management Tactics	Success Monitoring
Administra-tion	Classroom Set-Up	Group Size	Variety of Strategies	Managing Tools, i.e. Signals	Individual Accounta-bility
Parents	Teacher Materials	Hetero-geneous Grouping	Structured Tasks	Class Guidelines	Group Accounta-bility
Students	Student Materials	Group Processing Methods	Team Roles	Targeted Social Skills	Rewards, Incentives Celebrations
					Figure 12

Designs

A high school French teacher had just taken several training sessions in cooperative learning. It came time for her to teach the vocabulary for parts of the head to her first-year class. She paired her students and had each draw the outline of the other's head on a piece of butcher paper. Then, they wrote the correct French word for hair, eyes, nose, ears, lips, mouth, cheek, and so forth on each other's drawn head. She proudly displayed some samples and reported how quickly they had learned the vocabulary.

During her unit on the environment, an elementary teacher suggested a number of animals threatened with extinction. She divided the class into groups, and each one chose to study one of the threatened animals. During each group's report, each person in the group modeled how the animal behaved, dressing as closely as they could to look like the animal. The class was intrigued and attentive throughout all of the presentations.

This chapter is divided into three parts, corresponding to the three smaller circles shown in Figure 13. The first part describes some highly interactive designs that can be used with the entire class. These whole class designs might be a way to introduce cooperative learning to a class. The second part describes four designs to use in pairing situations. These might be the next step in getting a class acclimated to more interactive learning. The third part describes designs appropriate to the size of most high-functioning cooperative learning groups—three or four students.

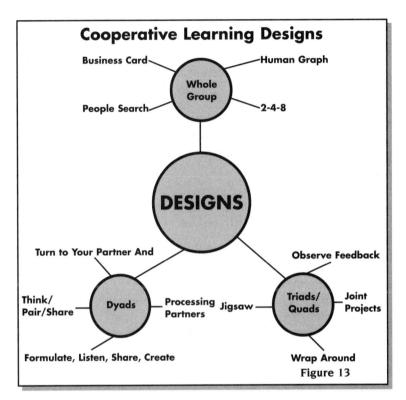

Cooperative Learning Designs

Business Card — Whole Group — Human Graph

People Search — 2-4-8

DESIGNS

Turn to Your Partner And — Observe Feedback

Think/ Pair/Share — Dyads — Processing Partners — Jigsaw — Triads/ Quads — Joint Projects

Formulate, Listen, Share, Create — Wrap Around

Figure 13

Whole Class

Even before using pair designs, teachers introducing cooperative learning might try some whole class cooperative learning designs in order to acquaint the class with different approaches to learning (Figure 13). Following the use of these designs, the teacher might ask some reflective questions about how students felt about the designs. This shared reflection helps the teacher determine how ready students are to proceed to more complex cooperative learning designs.

Business Card Design

Bellanca and Fogarty, in *Blueprints for Thinking in the Cooperative Classroom*, describe a design they call the business card (1991, p. 32). This design can be used as a great icebreaker at the beginning of a semester, allowing students and teachers to get to know each other. It is also a useful strategy to help teach information connected to any content area.

If using this design as an icebreaker activity, pass out 3 X 5 cards and have each student put his or her name in the center of the card. Select four categories that give information about the person: for example, hobby, talent, or skill; favorite actor/actress; favorite musical group; place they like to go on vacation; a phobia; and so forth. Next, ask students to write their personal responses for each of the four categories in the appropriate corner of their cards. Then, have students circulate around the room, sharing one of the corners with a classmate before moving on to share the contents of a different corner with another student. Figure 14 is an example of such an icebreaker or mixer card.

Business Card Sample #1:
Icebreaker or Mixer

Place I Like To Go On   Phobia
Vacation

NAME

Favorite Musical Group   Hobby, Talent
or Actor   or Skill

Figure 14

If using this design to help teach content, a math teacher could put an answer in the middle and ask students to create four ways to come up with that answer. Or, as shown in Figure 15, an English teacher could put the name of a character in the middle and, in the corners, four categories such as physical characteristics, character traits, major happenings or scenes in which the character played a major role, and the resolution that occurred for the character. Again, students circulate among their classmates and either share or ask for the information from another student.

Business Card Sample #2: Comprehension Strategy

Resolution, How The
Character Ends In The Story

Physical
Characteristics

NAME

Major Roles/Events
In The Story

Character
Traits

Figure 15

Before beginning a unit, many teachers have used this design to check out what their students already know about the unit topic. This is also a good way to hold a review before a test. Various topics could go into the center, with students filling out what they know about each topic and then circulating around the class, sharing information. The teacher could monitor the initial filling out of the cards to ensure accurate data is being recorded and shared.

People Search

Bellanca and Fogarty, in *Blueprints for Thinking in the Cooperative Classroom* (1991, pp. 49, 291), and Fogarty, in *Designs for Cooperative Interactions* (1990, pp. 34-7) include this design for the whole class. Pass out 3 X 5 cards; have each student draw a line down the middle and two lines across to make six boxes on the card. On an overhead, list six items or questions (see Figure 16 for an example of items about World War I). Then, have students circulate and find a student peer who fits the category. In other words, students are to find other students who can respond to one of the six items. Suggest that when a student answers or responds to one of the items, that student signs his or her name in the appropriate box on the 3 X 5 card. After talking to one classmate, students go on to another student so they don't have more than one signature per student peer.

Other items that have worked in a people search look like this:

Find someone who can list the four main characters of _____ story.

Find someone who can list the steps of the scientific method.

Find someone who can make up a different ending to the play we just studied.

Find someone who can solve this problem in a different way.

Find someone who agrees or disagrees with the author's conclusion.

People Search Example # 1: World War I

Name three causes to WWI.	Explain why the USA entered WWI.
Imagine what would have happened if the USA had not entered the war.	Name three famous generals from WWI.
Explain how WWI influenced the formation of the league of nations.	Imagine what would have happened if the league of nations had not been formed.

Figure 16

Be sure to include questions that require different thinking skill levels, that is, some questions that call for prescribed answers and some questions that require thought and could have any of several answers.

People search is a great way to review for a test. It can highlight important facts, pose thoughtful questions, and serve as a quick recap of the topic. For example, a people search about the November 2000, election might look like Figure 17.

People Search Example # 2: U.S. Election, 2000

Find Someone Who Can...

Name six important figures in the November 2000 Election.	Explain why the race was so close.
Interpret Gore's reasons for holding out as long as he did before conceding.	Predict what would have happened if the Supreme Court had not shut down the recount of votes.
Name four key issues of the campaign.	List a six-point plan for guaranteeing that such a controversial situation never happens again.

Figure 17

Human Graph

Bellanca and Fogarty, in *Blueprints for Thinking in the Cooperative Classroom* (1991, pp. 147, 153, 159–160, 335), and Fogarty, in *Designs for Cooperative Interactions* (1990, pp. 42–5), describe the human graph as another good design for the whole class. This is an excellent design for initiating discussions or debates about highly controversial issues.

Using the wall, the teacher posts cards that show several different opinions about a particular topic. The opinions range from highly positive through neutral to highly negative. Five to eight different opinions give students a good selection. Then, with the whole class present, ask students to stand next to the card that most represents their opinion on the topic, forming a line. Forming lines in front of the opinion cards is more revealing than raising hands in class: it requires movement and risk taking by each student and it shows the spectrum of opinion in the class in a highly visible way.

Several activities easily follow from this design. A little math can be interjected by creating a bar graph showing the numbers of students selecting each opinion. The members of groups for each opinion might get together to look for data to justify that opinion, form a debating team, or present support for the opinion to the class. At the end of the planned activities for this topic, check the spectrum of opinion again: ask students to line up under the opinion they have now, and to share why they changed their opinion or why they didn't.

Figure 18 shows an example of using the human graph design. It is easy to see how much research could go into creating a well-documented presentation of one of these points.

Human Graph: U.S. Energy Crisis

The energy crisis is creating concern about finding alternative oil supplies that do not depend on the Middle Eastern countries. One suggestion is to drill for oil in the Alaskan Wild Refuge Preserves. The range of opinions on this suggestion might be:

(1) We need the oil. Do what it takes to get it.

(2) We need the oil. Create strict guidelines that must be followed in order to get the oil.

(3) We've already hurt Alaska's wildlife with the Exxon Valdez incident. Don't touch the preserve.

(4) Only touch the preserve if the Middle East cuts off our oil supply.

(5) We have precious few protected places left in this country. Don't touch the preserve.

Arrange cards along a line on a wall with short descriptions of each opinion:

_____	(1)	What it takes
_____	(2)	Create strict guidelines
_____	(3)	Neutral
_____	(4)	Only use preserve if
_____	(5)	Do not touch the preserve

Figure 18

2-4-8

Fogarty, in *Designs for Cooperative Interactions* (1990, pp. 26–9), includes this design that combines the pair, a group of four, and a larger group of eight. Although this makes it one of the more complex designs to carry out, it is also one of the most rewarding to implement. It is a very appropriate design to use after a teacher has assigned individual students a small project, such as writing a poem or a paragraph, solving a word problem, coming up with a design for something, creating the plot for a short story, and so forth.

After individual work is completed, the class forms pairs. Person A in the pair shares what he or she has completed with the other person, person B. Then, person B shares what he or she has completed with person A. A couple of minutes for each person is ample time usually.

Then, ask each pair to join another pair to make groups of four. This time, person A shares what his or her partner, person B, came up with. Likewise, person C shares what his partner, Person D, came up with. In turn, person B shares what person A came up with, and person D shares what person C came up with. About a minute and a half for each person is probably enough time.

Next, ask each group of four to join another group of four to make a group of eight. In this round, person A shares what person C or person D created. Person C or D shares what person A or B created, and so on. In other words, at every step, each person is sharing something different. In this round, only a minute or so is needed for each person.

To recap total timing for the 2-4-8 design: four minutes for the first round, six minutes for the second, and eight minutes for the third. Adding a few extra minutes for shifting groups and for those groups that take longer, twenty to twenty-five minutes should be enough time.

Even if a class doesn't break into multiples of eight, this design can still work by allowing groups to be creative. When the entire design is completed, allow students time to jot down ideas that have come to them as they heard their peers' presentations. Then, of course, reflect with them about what they got out of the design.

Usually, people are excited to hear so many creative ideas. Needless to say, this design requires a number of social skills, including taking turns and attentive listening. In addition, a number of critical thinking skills are demanded, including the ability to summarize and prioritize what to put into a short minute or minute-and-a-half presentation.

This design works well when the class is asked to bring in something they have been working on since the last class. Then, the 2-4-8 becomes a forum for sharing that tangible item with their peers.

Dyads

These are some of the simplest designs to try in the classroom. Some of these only use a couple of minutes. For those teachers who are afraid to change the way the class is controlled, using these designs may give confidence that even more complex designs might work in their classroom. Figure 13 shows several designs for using dyads in cooperative learning.

Turn to Your Partner And . . .(TTYPA . . .)

Fogarty, in *Designs for Cooperative Interactions* (1990, pp. 10–3), offers this design as one of the simplest to do in the classroom. It's an excellent strategy to introduce the class to a more interactive approach. One way to use it is after a short lecture, video, or team presentation. Have everyone turn to a partner and recite five things they remember from what has just been heard. After each person recites to his or her partner, everyone returns to the whole group. The teacher might at that point ask the whole group to share some of the things they remembered.

Figure 19 shows a few other examples of appropriate times to use the turn to your partner and . . . design.

Examples of Using Turn To Your Partner And . . .

Turn to your partner and

share four of the most important points from the video.

recall three things that interested you most from the team presentation we just heard.

mention four things from the first part of the lecture and then have your partner mention four things from the second part of the lecture.

Figure 19

Think/Pair/Share

Fogarty, in Designs for Cooperative Interactions (1990, pp. 18–21), offers this design involving a little more complexity than the turn to your partner and . . . design. First, each person is asked to think through a particular idea. Second, each person shares his or her thinking with the partner. Third, the partners dialogue about what each has said. Then, they integrate their thinking into something more refined or more complex and give a shared answer.

For example, have students get in pairs. Each student thinks individually for a minute about why the girl in the story decided to carry out her plan in the way she did. Then, have each student share his or her thinking with a partner. Next, ask partners to decide together on the best reason for the character's actions, and be ready to report it in eight minutes with their explanation of why they chose that reason.

Formulate, Listen, Share, Create

Johnson, Johnson, and Holubec, in Cooperation in the Classroom (1998, pp. 1.36, 2.22), suggest the structure of formulate, share, listen, and create for use in a pairing situation. To begin, each student *formulates* an answer to a question or problem posed by the teacher. Then, each student *shares* his or her thoughts with a partner. It is important that each student *listen* carefully to what the partner has articulated so that, together, they can *create* a response that is better than either of the individual responses. This design emphasizes the necessity of listening and pushes the students' higher order thinking by asking them to create a response better than either of their individual ones. This design adds a little more complexity to

Think/Pair/Share by pushing for something specific to be created after the sharing has occurred.

An example of this design might have students choose a partner and formulate a response around the question "How did the climate influence the life style and the culture of (country)?" Have students take a minute to work on this individually. Then, have them share with a partner, reminding them to listen carefully to what each says. Finally, ask them to create together an answer that uses both of their thinking.

Processing Partners (Chapman's workshop sessions)

This is another dyad design that enables student reflection and processing. Processing partners are designated and kept for a long period of time— perhaps a month or so. Unlike a neighboring partner in the turn to your partner and . . . design, a processing partner may be someone on the other side of the room. Processing partners get together from time to time throughout their partnership to help each other process material being learned. It is important that teachers give short processing assignments; it allows partners to stand while they process (see Figure 20 for some examples). Therefore, a processing assignment becomes a wonderful short, structured activity allowing the students to move around the room.

Examples of Assignments for Processing Partners

Tell each other the most helpful part of this lesson for you.

Share three things that you want to be sure and remember from the lesson today.

Share three practical applications out of the science experiment performed today.

Come up with two reasons why it is important to know about the mathematical process we worked on today.

Figure 20

Triads/Quads

After a class has done some initial social skills training and has used some pairing or whole class designs, it's ready to try more complex triad or quad designs (Figure 13). Such a design is often used to complete a specific task or project, such as filling out a graphic organizer or creating a team presentation on a particular topic. In these designs, it is helpful to use team roles such as organizer, encourager, materials handler, recorder, timekeeper, and so forth (see Figure 9 for a list of useful roles).

If these group designs don't work well right away, a class may need more work in social skills training (see the next chapter) or more experiences with dyads or whole class strategies. This may be new for both teacher and students because the teacher is training the class in new ways of learning.

Observer Feedback

Fogarty, in *Designs for Cooperative Interactions* (1990, pp. 22–5), offers observer feedback as a variation on the think/pair/share design. A third student is added to the think/pair/share dyad to carry out an observer role. The observer notes how the skill or process is being carried out, which permits the pair to become involved fully in whatever the skill or process is. Meanwhile, the observer has just one job—monitoring how one group member carries out the skill or process and how the second member responds to the skill or process.

This is a particularly helpful design when teaching a skill or a process. For example, a math teacher might use it to teach long division. To start, the teacher divides the class into groups of threes. Within in each group, students are designated as person A, B, and C, each of whom has a specific role. Person A is to instruct person B on how to solve a long division problem. Person B is to carry out Person A's instructions. Person C is to note how well person A is instructing and how well person B is following the instructions. When done, Person C gives feedback to both Person A and Person B. On the next round, roles are switched, so that Person A observes, Person B instructs, and Person C carries out the instructions.

Jigsaw

Johnson, Johnson, and Holubec, in *Cooperation in the Classroom* (1998, p. 2.25), describe the jigsaw design as a way to help a class to get on top of a lot of information and material. Students have been assigned to cooperative groups, whose number and size depend on the topic. The teacher divides the topic or the reading material among the cooperative groups, giving a reasonable chunk to each group (this is why the number of groups depends on the topic). Then, the teacher further divides each subtopic or material into reasonable chunks, which are chosen or assigned to individual group members (this is why the size of the group also depends on the material). Each student becomes expert on his or her subtopic, and then teaches it to the others in the group or works with the group to create a team presentation. At some point, the groups have an opportunity to share their work. If the jigsaw work extends over several lessons, assigning group roles is particularly crucial to ensure the group's functioning well.

For example, if a class is studying the United States, each cooperative group might study a different region, such as the Northeast, the Middle Atlantic, the Southeast, the Midwest, the Southwest, or the Northwest. Then, individual group members might cover different features of a region, such as its economics, its politics (including state breakdowns, capitols, political leanings, etc.), its population and demographics, or its notable cultural aspects.

Joint Projects

Johnson, Johnson, and Holubec, in *Cooperation in the Classroom* (1998, p. 2.34), also talk about a design called a "joint project." Cooperative groups of three or four are assigned a particular project to work on—for example, creating a graphic organizer summarizing some reading material. Each student in the group might use a different colored pen so that when the organizer is finished, the teacher knows which student contributed which pieces of information. When the joint project is completed, each student signs his or her name, showing that all of the students participated in the joint project.

For example, a science teacher might use this design after cooperative learning groups have completed a scientific experiment. The teacher asks each group to draw the steps they followed in the experiment on chart paper, and to create a web of the practical implications or practical applications growing out of the experiment. Each student signs his or her name at the bottom of the chart.

Wrap-Around

Fogarty, in *Designs for Cooperative Interactions* (1990, pp. 38–41), includes this design as a quick way to get everyone's participation. This activity can be done as a whole class by asking for quick short responses. To accommodate longer responses, it can be done by having smaller groups simultaneously do wrap-arounds. In this design, everyone has a chance to say something within a very short amount of time.

For example, a teacher asks each cooperative learning group to do a wrap-around so that members may share their thoughts about the deeper messages from a poem they studied. After the groups have done this wrap-around, the teacher asks each group, "What are some of the messages people shared?" With these two wrap-arounds, each student had a chance to participate (in the cooperative learning group), and the teacher gets a feel for the kind of thinking going on in the class (from the responses of each group in the whole class).

Developments

A middle school used the morning classes before lunch to teach the standard curriculum. There was some effort at cooperative learning in the regular classes of math, language arts, social sciences, and science taught by the four teachers. After lunch, all of the students were divided into interest groups. In this session, all four teachers checked on the groups and on how the projects were going. They had the advantage of a huge room in which some students were working on a computer, others were making models of something studied in language arts, and still others were carrying out their business plan for a small company they were starting as part of a social science project. There were ten or eleven groups all heavily engaged in work. Each person carried out an assigned role and an assigned task, so each group exhibited a smooth flow of cooperation and interaction. Leadership, consensus, teamwork, and communication were happening at once.

One of the key benefits to students as they gain more experience in cooperative learning is the acquisition and perfecting of needed social skills. As with any content subject, social skills develop step-by-step over time. Students who have underdeveloped social skills do not suddenly acquire them overnight, just as course content is not learned overnight. As Figure 21 shows, there are four big skills that are important for cooperative learning: leading, generating consensus, building a team, and communicating.

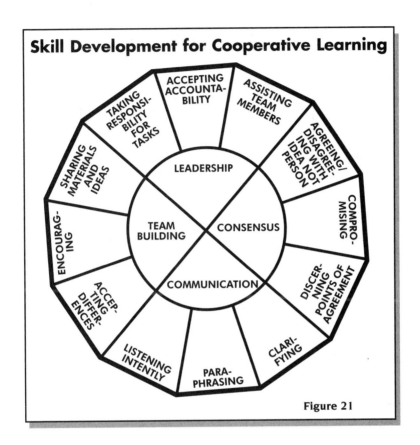

Skill Development for Cooperative Learning

ACCEPTING ACCOUNTA-BILITY

ASSISTING TEAM MEMBERS

TAKING RESPONSI-BILITY FOR TASKS

AGREEING/ DISAGREE-ING WITH IDEA NOT PERSON

SHARING MATERIALS AND IDEAS

LEADERSHIP

COMPRO-MISING

ENCOURAG-ING

TEAM BUILDING

CONSENSUS

COMMUNICATION

DISCER-NING POINTS OF AGREEMENT

ACCEP-TING DIFFER-ENCES

LISTENING INTENTLY

PARA-PHRASING

CLARI-FYING

Figure 21

Leading

Leading refers to the master skills shown in Figure 22. In the world of work, these skills are more and more important in the growing environment of teams.

Master Skills for Leading

Taking responsibility for tasks

Accepting some form of accountability for the completion of tasks

Offering assistance to team members to enable them to finish a task

Figure 22

Cooperative learning groups offer an opportunity for students to experience various kinds of leadership roles in a relatively safe and supportive environment—an environment constantly monitored by the classroom teacher. In the beginning, group roles are clearly defined, and the tasks are specific. As time goes on, tasks grow in complexity. Leading a group in creating a graphic organizer gradually grows into leading a group to create a several-week-long science project on the solar system.

All of this helps the student who may feel intimidated or shy in group situations. Leadership roles in a group of three, four, or five can often give the student confidence to assume leadership roles with larger groups of students.

Generating Consensus

Generating consensus refers to the master skills shown in Figure 23. Diversity is becoming an ever-present quality in business and social situations. It takes great skill to pull together differing perspectives into points of agreement.

Master Skills for Generating Consensus

Agreeing or disagreeing with an idea, not a person

Compromising

Discerning points of agreement and consensus in team discussions

Figure 23

It is fortunate that schools represent the same diversity encountered throughout society. Cooperative learning groups become laboratories for learning how to honor and work with a variety of perspectives and strengths. When groups of students are assigned controversial topics, it gives them an opportunity to discover how to express passionate support or strong disgust for ideas rather than getting upset with the individuals holding those ideas. The successful execution of cooperative tasks calls for compromises and also for discipline to discern the points of agreement within the points of disagreement.

The master skills in generating consensus are the positive expressions of skills needed in conflict management. One way to manage conflict is by helping people recognize connections they didn't know were there. These days, anger and violence are a real, though unfortunate, part of school life. Working in cooperative groups helps students build skills in solving problems and building connections that offer them alternatives beyond anger and violence. In this way, cooperative learning supports other efforts, such as peer mediation, in creating more supportive school environments for all students.

Building a Team

Building a team refers to the master skills shown in Figure 24. Although teachers may wish that students came to the classroom well-experienced in these skills, the reality is that in an age of TV, computers, mobility, and reduced time with busy working parents, many students need explicit help in the classroom to learn them.

Master Skills in Building a Team

Sharing materials and ideas

Encouraging with appropriate comments and gestures

Accepting the different skills and perspectives in the team

Figure 24

Skilled ability in building teams is especially needed today because the work world often is composed of work teams. It is invaluable for students heading for the world of work to have had experience in classroom teams. When cooperative learning is implemented well in the classroom, students have a chance to experience opportunities to share, encourage, and accept. In these situations, students learn first hand that tasks are done better and more smoothly when accompanied with sharing, encouragement, and acceptance.

One way a teacher can structure this skill is by offering each group only one set of materials and equipment. This pushes the students to find ways to share, encourage, and accept.

Communicating

Communicating refers to the master skills shown in Figure 25. These communicating skills have become incisive in the work world as it becomes both more team-oriented and more global and diverse.

Master Skills for Communicating

Listening intently

Paraphrasing concisely

Clarifying with well-chosen questions

Figure 25

Cooperative learning often requires discussion, problem solving, and decision making. All of these require students to listen, paraphrase, and clarify in order to finish whatever task they have been assigned. Often this calls for the teacher to embed the need for communication within the particular task or problem assigned to the group. In this way, the teacher makes the task complex enough that listening, paraphrasing, and clarifying are required in order to complete the assignment.

For example, a reading is divided into sections, which are given to individuals in the group to complete. Completion calls for each individual to read the section assigned and prepare a way to convey the material to the others in the group. In turn, this calls for others in the group to listen, paraphrase, and clarify to make sure they have grasped the essential content that their peer has just read and taught them.

Improving Social Skills

Cooperative group learning is one way for needed social skills to be taught and experienced. This is the milieu in which life skills are introduced and practiced. Teachers need to become adept at both teaching the skills directly and embedding skills within classroom lessons.

Teaching a Social Skill Directly

Certain steps are helpful in making sure the social skill gets taught well (Figure 26).

Steps in Teaching a Social Skill Directly

Call attention to the skill.	Practice, practice, practice.
Demonstate the skill.	Monitor.
Teach explicitly.	Celebrate.
Operationalize the skill.	

Figure 26

Calling attention to the skill spotlights the skill to be taught. Sometimes, a video may demonstrate the skill being performed well or poorly. Sometimes, role playing a situation might work. Then, teaching the skill is important. Actually describing it is often necessary. Operationalize the social skill by talking through what it sounds like and looks like—this can make it very real.

After the skill is clear to the class, it's time for practice and more practice. While practice is going on, the teacher moves around and monitors progress. Finally, the teacher might find some way to celebrate the successful learning of the skill.

Embedding Social Skill Development in a Regular Lesson

The second way to help students learn social skills is to embed social skills into regular lessons so that social skills get utilized more and more in regular classroom activities. For example, following a short lecture, a teacher might ask students to pair up and tell each other three things remembered from the lecture. This strengthens the skill of listening without taking much time.

Again, after a team assignment, a teacher might ask each team to reflect about how well they shared materials and ideas and rate their performance on a scale of one to ten. Then, the teacher might ask for a quick report from each team. This doesn't take much time, but it reinforces a social skill within a regular lesson or assignment.

Closing

Each of the four chapters of this book have responded to ongoing concerns relative to cooperative learning. **Description** defines cooperative learning and outlines some of the theoretical perspectives that have laid the foundation for the many tools teachers use today in implementing cooperative learning.

Decisions acquaints teachers with areas to consider and with decisions they need to make to carry out cooperative learning effectively in their classrooms. This chapter might even assist those who have already been using cooperative learning to deepen its impact.

Designs offers a number of cooperative learning strategies and tools. This chapter suggests a flow for the teacher—what to begin with and then what might be more appropriate as the teacher and students gain more experience with cooperative learning in the classroom.

Developments enumerates some of the social skill impacts that cooperative learning can have when it is used well in the classroom. Society and the business world have come to see how crucial social skills are in the growth and development of students.

Students come to school with broadened perspectives and deepened expectations. Media, music, and movies produce students ready to be taken seriously. School these days needs to make sense to every student who walks into the classroom. The opportunity to interact responsibly with peers makes sense to students. The opportunity to interact dynamically with peers heightens the motivation to learn. The opportunity to engage profoundly in relevant, challenging material communicates how much the teacher respects the growing minds and forming opinions of those in the classroom.

I would welcome your comments as you offer this opportunity of cooperative learning to your students.

Bibliography

Astuto, T. A., Clark, D. L., Read, A. M., McGree, K., & Fermandez, L. D. P. (1994). *Roots of reform: Challenging the assumptions that control change in education.* Bloomington, IN: Phi Delta Kappa Educational Foundation.

Augustine, D. K., Bruger, K. D., & Hanson, L. R. (1989). Cooperation works! *Educational Leadership,* 47(4), 4–7.

Bellanca, J., & Fogarty, R. (2004). *Blueprints for thinking in the cooperative classroom.* Thousand Oaks, CA: Corwin Press.

Burke, K. (Ed.). (1995). *Managing the interactive classroom: A collection of articles.* Thousand Oaks, CA: Corwin Press.

Caine, G., Caine, R. N., & Crowell, S. (1994). *Mindshifts: A brain-based process for restructuring schools and renewing education.* Tucson, AZ: Zephyr Press.

Caine, R. N., & Caine, G. (1991). *Making connections: Teaching and the human brain.* Alexandria, VA: Association for Supervision and Curriculum Development.

Caine, R. N., & Caine, G. (1997a). *Education on the edge of possibility.* Alexandria, VA: Association for Supervision and Curriculum Development.

Caine, R. N., & Caine, G. (1997b). *Unleashing the power of perceptual change.* Alexandria, VA: Association for Supervision and Curriculum Development.

Costa, A. L. (1991). *The school as home for the mind.* Thousand Oaks, CA: Corwin Press.

Costa, A. L., & Kallick, B. (2000). *Habits of mind.* Alexandria,VA: Association for Supervision and Curriculum Development.

Fogarty, R. (1990). *Designs for cooperative interactions.* Thousand Oaks, CA: Corwin Press.

Fogarty, R. (1994). *Teach for metacognitive reflection.* Palatine, IL: Skylight Training and Publishing.

Fogarty, R. (1995). *Best practices for the learner-centered classroom.* Arlington Heights, IL: Skylight Training and Publishing.

Fogarty, R. (2001a). *Differentiated learning: Different strokes for different folks.* Chicago, IL: Fogarty & Associates.

Fogarty, R. (2001b). *Making sense of the research on the brain and learning.* Chicago, IL: Fogarty & Associates.

Fogarty, R. (2001c). *Standards of learning: A blessing in disguise.* Chicago, IL: Fogarty & Associates.

Fogarty, R. (2002). *Brain compatible classrooms* (2nd ed.). Thousand Oaks, CA: Corwin Press.

Fogarty, R., & Bellanca, J. (1991). *Patterns for thinking, patterns for transfer.* Palatine, IL: Skylight Publishing.

Fogarty, R., Perkins, D., & Barell, J. (1992). *How to teach for transfer.* Arlington Heights, IL: Skylight Training and Publishing.

Glasser, W. (1986). *Control theory in the classroom.* New York: Harper & Row.

Glickman, C. D. (2000). Holding sacred ground: The impact of standardization. *Educational Leadership, 58*(4), 46–51.

Goleman, D. (1995). *Emotional intelligence.* New York: Bantam Books.

Johnson, D. W., Johnson, R. T., & Holubec, E.J. (1986). *Circles of learning: Cooperation in the classroom.* Alexandria, VA: Association for Supervision and Curriculum Development.

Johnson, D. W., Johnson, R. T., & Holubec, E. J. (1998). *Cooperation in the classroom* (7th ed.). Edina, MN: Interaction Book.

Kagan, S. (1989). Cooperation works! *Educational Leadership*, 47(4), 12–15.

LeDoux, J. (1996). *The emotional brain*. New York: Touchstone.

Lyman, L., Foyle, H. C., & Azwell, T. S. (1993). *Cooperative learning in the elementary classroom.* Washington, DC: National Education Association.

Parry, T., & Gregory, G. (2003). *Designing brain compatible learning* (2nd ed.). Thousand Oaks, CA: Corwin Press.

Schniedewind, N., & Davidson, E. (2000). Differentiating cooperative learning. *Educational Leadership*, 58(1), 24–27.

Sharan, Y., & Sharan, S. (1989). Group investigation expands cooperative learning. *Educational Leadership*, 47(4), 17–21.

Silberman, M. (1996). *Active learning: 101 strategies to teach any subject.* Boston: Allyn and Bacon.

Slavin, R. E. (1987. Cooperative learning and the cooperative school. *Educational Leadership*, 45(3), 7–13.

Slavin, R. E. (1989). Cooperative learning models for the 3 R's. *Educational Leadership*, 47(4), 22–28.

Slavin, R. E. (1991). Synthesis of research on cooperative learning. *Educational Leadership*, 48(5), 71–82.

Sousa, D. (2006). *How the brain learns* (3rd ed.). Thousand Oaks, CA: Corwin Press.

Sylwester, R. (1995). *A celebration of neurons: An educator's guide to the human brain.* Alexandria, VA: Association for Supervision and Curriculum Development.

Tomlinson, C. (1999). *The differentiated classroom: Responding to the needs of all learners.* Alexandria, VA: Association for Supervision and Curriculum Development.

Tomlinson, C. (2000). Reconcilable differences? Standards-based teaching and differentiation. *Educational Leadership, 58*(1), 6–11.

U. S. Department of Labor. (1992). *Learning a living: A blueprint for high performance: A SCANS report for America 2000.* Washington, DC: U.S. Government Printing Office.

Wheatley, M. J. (1992). *Leadership and the new science.* San Francisco: Berrett-Koehler.

Zemelman, S., Daniels, H., & Hyde, A. (1993). *Best practice: New standards for teaching and learning in America's schools.* Portsmouth, NH: Heinemann.

CORWIN
PRESS

The Corwin Press logo—a raven striding across an open book—represents the union of courage and learning. Corwin Press is committed to improving education for all learners by publishing books and other professional development resources for those serving the field of PreK–12 education. By providing practical, hands-on materials, Corwin Press continues to carry out the promise of its motto: **"Helping Educators Do Their Work Better."**